Cultivated Time

Rose Willow

Copyright © 2020 by Rose Willow

All rights reserved. No part of this publication may be reproduced or transmitted in any form or by any means, electronic or mechanical, including photocopying, recording or any information storage or retrieval system, without permission in writing from the author.

Rose Willow, 1943-

ISBN 978-0-997449-7-6-1
1st edition

1. Canadian Poetry
2. Willow, Rose. Title

Cover photography: Anthony Hutchins

Weaver of Words Publishers
1056 Mallard Place
Qualicum Beach, British Columbia
word.weaver@shaw.ca

For my beloved, Anthony Hutchins, who stands by me through everything, and for my mother, Annie Gransch, (1921-2014), who always cared.

A poem is the past that breaks out of our hearts.
—Rilke

CONTENTS

Canada's Bread Basket 1
    In This New Land 3
    Horseradish 4
    Canada's Bread Basket 5
    Another Cigarette 6
    Contrition 7
    Relief Train 8
    Grandmother 9
    Dying Blue 10
    Cake Baked and Square Danced 11
    Cultivated Time 12
The Two of Them 13
    While My Father Dies 15
    Walked 16
    Wristwatch 17
    Paper Butterflies 18
    The Two of Them 19
    Snow Tunnels 20
    Across the Tracks 21
    Hands of a Working Man 22
    Coyotes 23
    Alfred Hitchcock 24
    Battleford 25
    Shucking 26

Swim Knitting 27
   Slats 29
   The Best Spellers 30
   Winter Boots 31
   At the Convent of St. Katharina 32
   Red and Yellow 33
   Sleepwalker 34
   A Higher Social Level 35
   Winter 36
   Mount Carmel 37
   Gossip 38
   Swim Knitting 39
What if 41
   Axle Alley 43
   Screw Driver's Retreat 44
   Low and Slow 45
   Pennies 46
   Crocheting Yoga 47
   Send Off 48
   Green Notebook 49
   Risk 50
   Fur Trimmed 51
   Capitalism 52
   Big Fat Purses 53
   Dwindling 54
   What if 55
Where Rests the Heart 57
   Sugar and Lime 59
   Sofa in Spice 60
   Toothpaste 61

- Beach Slippers...........62
- Breakfast...........63
- Fly Swatter...........64
- One Breath...........65
- Handkerchief...........66
- Night Waters...........67
- Where Rests the Heart...........68

Acknowledgements...........71
About the Author...........73

Canada's Bread Basket

In This New Land
For my maternal great grandparents who arrived in Canada in 1912

He cradles the bundle from the midwife and walks through the gate. No point in a trip to town. Why get a certificate for one who never lived; one unbaptized, and not allowed in hallowed ground? Who needs to spend ten dollars when the horses need new harness?

He digs near the alkali slough, draws deep on a cigarette, and examines the bundle. Another son he drops in the ground. He scans
this private graveyard – a third son. Surely God must understand how a man needs a son, how a man fails his ancestors, how a man mourns alone in this new land.

He fills the shovel and spills soil over the bundle; unmarked, the site looks almost undisturbed. He walks back towards the gate.

His four daughters call from across the field, "Papa, Papa, the chicks are hatched; quick come see."

He hopes for hens.

Horseradish
For my maternal Great grandparents

I am horseradish, cultivated since antiquity. I came with Mijat and Marya from Eastern Europe. Like prairie sun and wind, summer dust, and winter snow, I irritate sinuses and eyes. My roots are used for condiments; enhance the taste of beef and pork. My roots combined with my foliage provide medicine, and powerful poultices for ailments. But, Marya turned her back on ancient tradition, chose instead the modern way.

I watched the dust roil up behind the car as it marked the progress of the doctor's call. Her womb contracted with each scream of pain. The doctor used ether, a touch too much; she never woke up, her son never breathed.

The modern way got her an early grave. I remain in the far corner of what was their garden. All else is gone, the buildings, and fences. The prairie cultivated beyond recognition; I am the only trace that Mijat and Marya were ever here.

Canada's Bread Basket

Grain elevators, twenty-four meters high
with gabled cupolas atop gabled roofs,
painted CPR red, dot the prairie landscape
every twelve to sixteen kilometers
along the railway tracks.

Through the small dirty window in the cupola
a miniature town below is similar to many others,
the steeple of St. Martin's church the tallest building
nearby the school, hospital, and graveyard. Stores, shops,
a bank, post office, and two beer parlours, fill out
the centre. Tidy rows of houses run to the edge of town
in every direction, and hemmed in by Saskatoon berry
and Chokecherry bushes.

Gulls circle the nuisance grounds outside
the town's limits where two tattered army tents
shelter a small band of Cree
camped for two weeks a year.
Thin-blue smoke spirals from their campfire,
six or seven hobbled ponies
graze along the road.

All around wheat fields ripple in the wind.
Canada's bread basket – soil
the richest in the world.

Another Cigarette

the man without
legs pulled
the lid from

the tobacco can
pinched off
the right amount

carefully
spread across paper
rolled

into the grave yard
the smoky
hearse.

Contrition

The air close
The music heavy
The sermon too long

We stand

       sit

             kneel

                    mumble in Latin

                         Words we do not understand

We beat our breasts

       Once a week

              Failure means going to hell

                     Forever and forever and ever and ever

The air close
The music heavy
The sermon damned to be long

Relief Train
For Annie and Tina

The relief train pulled into the station, distributed supplies to the farmers, mostly feed for livestock; feed to keep a few cows, pigs, chickens, and horses alive. Dad always came home with feed, along with a little of something else. One time it was twelve cans of sardines, a box of over-ripe apples, and six pairs of high-heeled shoes.

Mother stretched the sardines; mashed them into the boiled potatoes. She added them to the dough for dumplings. Dumplings, that's what filled us up. We ate lots of dumplings. The apples were too mushy for apple sauce; she fed them to the pigs; said it would sweeten their pork.

Dad took the buck-saw to the shoes; sawed off the heels, and my mother, my sister, and I had shoes; two pairs each, a pair for at home; a pair for church.

The toes curled upwards, and the kids at school poked fun at us. *Here come those stupid girls, trying to ski when there is no snow.* I took to hiding mine in the ditch along the road and went bare-foot.
Others went barefoot too, and I fit right in.

A broken beer bottle, left over from a Saturday night's country dance, sliced into my foot. It bled and bled. The teacher had a job to stop the bleeding, wrapped it up in his dirty handkerchief, and sent me home

I picked up my shoes from the ditch, and hobbled home. Mother wanted to know how I could cut my foot on a broken beer bottle when I had shoes to wear on my feet. I told her I had taken them off so I could run faster around the bases of the ball diamond.

It was a lie, a little white lie, but like the relief train, it got us by.

Grandmother

Drudgery shuffled out the kitchen door
with a well dealt hand of solitaire.
She taught her grandchildren
how to play Deuces Wild and Schmier.
The waft of Jelly Roll and Date Squares
meant guests for Kaiser or Canasta.

The sound of a polka on the radio,
and all her troubles were gone.
She taught her grandchildren
how to dance the Two Step
and Old Time Waltz.
Her work-weary legs sprung
spritely at any country dance.

Dressed in her new blue dress,
hair and make-up perfect,
her hands clasped a prayer book
while a white-beaded rosary
meandered through her fingers.
The Hesitation Waltz soothed
as background music, and Uncle Paul
slipped a deck of cards
into grandmother's open casket.

Dying Blue

My mind swims with thoughts of cobalt
silvery-white like dental floss
slips through narrow passages
of darkness

Cobalt makes into deep blue pigment
glows the blue flame of propane
reflects through the broken
window

Granddad with sky blue eyes
behind old spectacles
sinks his last breath
a submarine.

Cake Baked and Square Danced

stone boat
in this new land
stalks sorrow
horse radish
in Canada's bread basket
another cigarette
before contrition
the relief train
before grandmother
dying blue, cake baked
and square danced
on treaty six lands

Cultivated Time

land wears thin on cultivated time
abandoned farm houses sag; top soil drifts
leaky rain barrels, life dribbles away

The Two of Them

While My Father Dies

I braid my hair
tight, like mother used to do

Tight, until it hurts
Tight, until every strand
is bound so tight
it pulls my scull.

I wait while my father dies.
Wait for his last breath.
Pain the perpetual red light,
in church, the presence
of Christ everlasting
pain – his and mine.

A ray of sunshine glimmers
through a stained glass window
a faint glow of love – everlasting – teeters
between heaven and earth—
tests the weight of us.

Walked

Above all, do not lose your desire to walk. Every day I walk myself into a state of well-being...I have walked myself into my best thoughts, and I know of no thought so burdensome that one cannot walk away from it.
Soren Kierkegaard

My father walked – the hills of Savona. Walked past ninety-seven. Walked until his legs wobbled; he couldn't lift his feet.

I walked – in circles around Lake Cowichan. Walked until my toe nails turned black; one by one, they fell out.

My father and I walked but not toward each other.

Wristwatch

Mother, can you hear me
when I visit your grave?
Do you know when I am there?

Do you feel cold?
I wish I had wrapped my quilt around you
before they closed the lid.

I don't like to think of you in your coffin;
dressed in your going-away outfit,
shoes and stockings, best underwear and bra,
hair brushed, make-up perfect, fingernails polished,
hands folded on your chest, fingers entwined with your rosary.

Glasses
    Dentures
        Wedding ring
            Wristwatch

Do you know what time it is? You used to ask when I came
home late as a teenager.

It bothers me; your wristwatch down there.
How long will it keep perfect time?
Would I hear it, if I pressed
my ear to the ground?

Paper Butterflies

You didn't need to know the history of Origami
or Froebel's "Kindergarten" method
to teach your children how to fold
paper hats, boats, airplanes.

Butterflies you saved for moments by yourself
folded glossy magazine pages into tight accordion
pleats; your foot tapping in time
to polkas on the gramophone.

Trees into paper, your heart's last flutter,
a purple Astor held in your hand,
paper butterflies stuck static on the wall.

The Two of Them

I pulled the quilt up over my head when he got home from the beer parlour. Mother shouted, *where were you, and what were you doing?* I heard him stagger and then slur his words about money he'd won in a poker game and another C.O.D. parcel, from Simpson's Sears, he'd left in the truck the night before. Mother said we needed food to put on the table, and new boots and coats for winter. We all needed a peaceful night's sleep before work and school the next morning. They argued all the way up the stairs and down the hallway. I burrowed further under my quilt; wished they would just – shut-up.

Snow Tunnels

It is 12 below Fahrenheit.
My brother and I scrape frost
from the window.
We play Snakes and Ladders,
Or build a house of cards with Daddy's favourite deck.
Or draw fence posts, grain fields,
pussy willows, and cat tails in inky blue sloughs.

At 10 below we are allowed to play outside.
Mom pulls Daddy's old socks up over our
pant legs to keep the snow out.
We wear double mittens.
Scarves, crisscrossed, a mummy wrap
around our heads and necks,
only our eyes and noses peek out.

We build an igloo.
It turns into a snow fort.
Then we dig a tunnel in the snow bank.
Daddy has warned us not to.
Says such tunnels can cave in and we
could suffocate. We do it anyway.

Our shovels strike something solid.
Snow bleeds purplish red, oozes
from a jug of Daddy's home brew.
We crawl into the snow tunnel.
Shiver thoughts
tonight's pending storm.

Across the Tracks

my first reading attempt
like mashed potatoes
or snow drifting
across the railway tracks

another baby brother
circumcised
coyotes howled
while mother
prayed the rosary

Mary Anne's coat
found down the
neighbour's
outdoor toilet hole

I asked for a pair
of white figure skates
and gave up
on Santa Claus

Hands of a Working Man

A round snuff box in a rough work shirt pocket, work pants held up by suspenders, in his mouth, either a tooth pick or a cigarette, sometimes a match stick, with always a few loose ones in his pocket. He could light a match with his thumb nail. Instead of a package of cigarettes, there might be cigarette papers and tobacco, a sign of whether times were good or bad. He had rough tough hands from cold hard work all day. My father's hands – hands of a working man. Hammer, level, measuring tape, a chisel or two, hung from the flaps and gussets of his coveralls. He used a tape measure; checked for accuracy, and then again, and sometimes again, once more.

Gruff all day, he barked orders to his crew; kicked any stray dog that dared lift a leg to chisel a yellow hole in winter's perfect snow bank. Saw-horses swayed in the back of his truck at the end of the day. A shot of whiskey or two, a glass of home brew, "Yeah, by golly, now I tell you, a man needs something besides working all day." After supper, he removed two rolls of elastic bandages from his varicose veined left leg; carefully rerolled; made ready for morning. ...and then, the click of knitting needles, a bag of wool beside his feet, he knit socks and mittens. One winter, he knitted a pull-over sweater just for me. It was burgundy with two pink ducks on front. He listened to his radio; found a Hit Parade....and then, the strokes of hair-brush, snarls and knots let loose, his soft caress, my father's hands – hands of a working man.

Coyotes

From our house at the edge of town,
we could see where prairie
meets sky. Sometimes, at dusk, I heard the
coyotes howl. The view from the kitchen window
scoped wider then Cineplex. The sound better
than Dolby or digital. But, I couldn't see
the coyotes no matter how long I waited.

The howls brought a night that darkened to a crescendo.
Mom closed the windows tight, lit the coal-oil lamp,
stuck a butcher knife in between the closed door
and frame. A freight train rumbled through,
whistled as it passed and then faded away.

On such nights Mom read us stories.
Of Peter Pan or Snow White or Cinderella
and her pumpkin coach.
We slept in the same bed,
my little brothers between my mother and me.
She turned on the radio to cover the sound of coyotes.
Under the quilt, my ear pressed the wall;
I imagined coyotes snuffling
around the corners of the house. I tried not
to think about Little Red Riding Hood, or
the Three Little Pigs – the huff and the puff.

Alfred Hitchcock

Alfred Hitchcock is over and I'm in bed
before mother turns off the TV, and shoos
my brothers off to their bedroom.
They scream,
"A man is looking in the window."
Mom runs to my brothers, yells
for me to phone the police.

They tell us that there are foot prints
in the flower bed, and that there have been
other reported sightings

Mother tells them her husband
works out of town, we belong to St. Mary's
parish, the children go to
St. Maria Goretti School,
that I'm the one who phoned them,
and that I'm a very good student.
She doesn't tell them one of my brothers isn't,
and one sometimes pees the bed

I too, want them to think we are a model
family, like in *Leave it to Beaver,*
My Three Sons, and *Father Knows Best.*
I don't want them to know our father
drinks, chases other women, and when
he is home belittles our mother,
beats my brothers, slips me money
before he leaves, and tells
me to buy myself something.

Battleford

I catch acorns when I stick out
my tongue by magic they drop
from the oak when I pass by
to wash my hair in the rain
barrel, and then roll
around on the chamomile lawn.
Inside, I bite a balloon, watch
the explosion on the wall,
some chicken
plucks a guitar, one leg in a
silk stocking. Arm tracks
punctured, a cat's claw
scrapped down, swept by
broomsticks, the chokecherry
juice drips black red.
Breakdown, some kind of trip.

Electric shock,
Smarten up, they say.
Well, you can't slice a raw egg
with a chain-saw, comb your
hair with an axe.
In the cocoon of isolation,
I can shrink as small
as a pea, hide under a mattress,
aggravate a foot in a shoe, know how
to avoid pea soup. I will again
grow tall, hiss fire, when next
the screw, opens the door.

Shucking

The coast, 1989:
I dig for clams with
a garden hoe.
You pry oysters off rocks,
with a wrecking bar.

The tide changes
spews spray across the rocks.
A sea monster
like some disgruntled warrior,
shows no mercy
to the hunter-gatherer.

I rake regret, a patch to scar
the ocean floor, as you
salvage half-full buckets
and retreat.

Hurricane forces
clammed up tight.
You shuck.
I steam.

Pour wine.
Measure carefully
our words
to one another.

Swim Knitting

Slats

Polio kept my nine month old baby brother in a hospital where at eleven I wasn't allowed to visit. I prayed for him; lit candles in church. After school, I often shivered outside on the hospital steps as October skies threatened snow and early winter. Sister Cecelia caught me crying and led me past reception. Reverent Mother looked the other way.

The scent of disinfectant followed me down a hallway. Polished tiles blurred beneath my scurrying feet. I heard the swish of Sister's stiff white apron, noticed the sway of her habit, and the close brown weave, I had always thought was black.

Sister guided me into a small white room with sunshine streaming through a casement window. A crucifix hung on a white wall over a high white crib. My baby brother wore a loose white gown. He was on his back; his left leg bent.

I slipped my hand through the slats of the crib. Our hands curled together; our eyes met, his smile held my heart.

The Best Spellers

The best spellers came out of our grade-seven class. The teacher's view, narrow as the aisles between our desks, anyone could make a mistake. Anything more would warrant the switch, for he cleaned the slate of lazy habits, with one stroke for each error over one. Spelling tests were held on Friday afternoons, every previous day haunted by reminders to study. Lessons, in the Spelling Text, consisted of ten pairs of words. Obstacles in a dangerous alley ready to pounce.

extinct   *century*   *celery*
succinct   *sentry*   *salary*

And then, lined up at the front of the class, in turn bent over the teacher's desk; once one of the boys had almost all of his wrong. None of us counted the number of strokes, but we saw him slump to the floor. His sobs cut the silence. One girl peed her pants, and I threw up. The teacher reminded us, that what went on in the classroom, behind the closed door, was private; a place like the confessional. If he ever heard that any of us had told, anything to anyone, we would get the same.

That weekend, Dad announced he had bought a house in Saskatoon. We would move in six weeks. I managed to be sick every Friday until then, and never became one of the best spellers.

Winter Boots

Saddle-Oxford shoes crunched on the hard packed sidewalk snow, the Saskatoon winter of 1957, when winter boots were out of style. So were thick brown winter stockings, and slacks weren't allowed either over or under our navy-blue uniforms. White Bobbie-socks griped snug around ankles, but the rest of our bare legs turned reddish-purple blue, the six block trek from the bus-stop. Standing beside our desks for morning prayers, our legs glowed red and tingled all the way up to only God knew where. Seated for Sister Marilyn's Religious Studies class our legs felt burnt, itched, and no one dared scratch.

One morning I slipped my thick brown winter stockings underneath my white Bobbie-socks, and hoped no one would notice. I got as far as the hallway before the silent sideways glances, the muffled snickers, and a pointed finger or two. Thoughts about my once frozen legs, felt mild compared to the cold disapproval of teenage girls.

At the Convent of St. Katharina

Sky, tight framed within
the bedroom window.
In the forefront, elms
gracious with their
shade, a wind stirs
flickers light
to dance the walls,
enters the room without
permission. A ghostly black
Habit, flows the hush of hallway.
A creak on cellar stairs, nature finds
a way of telling. Legitimate or not, secret
filled bellies, disguise their cautious tidings.

Red and Yellow

yellow light oozes
from streetlights
into the bedroom
the mattress sags
wallpaper peels

she cuts parts
of herself

red and yellow mix
to orange

Sleepwalker

The top of her nightgown gapes open. I grasp the cups of her bra; gasp to find them stuffed with soft plastic. She steps back, rolls her eyes at my pee-stained underwear, tries not to laugh, and proposes a toast. I slink towards the doorway; pretend I'm a sleepwalker.

A Higher Social Level

At the Royal Bank, men smoke cigarettes all day; the Bank Manager sucks on a pipe. Women aren't allowed to smoke in front of customers, which means from ten until three. The smoke thickens after three when they light up. I've quit because I'm pregnant and married or not, I won't be able to work here after I start to show.

We are salaried employees paid monthly with an advance in the middle of the month. We work eight hours a day, five days a week. There is no overtime if we stay late. Sometimes the supervisor, usually male, disappears at cash lock-up time, and us female tellers hang around and pretend we don't mind.

A cut above the hourly paid wage-earner, we are expected to look the part – skirts, dresses, nylon stockings, and shoes with respectable heels. Our hair is puffed-up and spray-netted; our faces made-up Hollywood perfect. The men wear suits, white shirts, and ties.

Men get more pay to start, and don't stay as tellers for long. A training program turns them into supervisors, personnel managers, assistant mangers, and Branch Managers. For women it's opportunity to mingle at a higher social level. I managed to snag a husband without dirt under his fingernails.

We gather after three o'clock the day I leave. Everyone lights up, and I feel nauseous from the smell of smoke and fresh brewed coffee. Plates of baked goodies are passed around. I'm presented with a little card signed by everyone. They say they are sorry to see me leave. The Branch Manager says a few words; offers no guarantee I can return.

Winter

wind whispers warnings
creeps under collars and cuffs
ends the summers of love

snow dogs prowl the sky
temperatures bead frozen
icicles don't melt

wind wails reckonings
swirls snow into drifts
blizzards their marriage

Mount Carmel
Humboldt Saskatchewan

The women arrive before the sun sets,
clamber from the base, trek
upwards along the Stations of the Cross,
one grasps a cluster of chokecherries.
Lingers the flush of day, the view sweeps
four hundred miles of horizon at the mound.

Soft darkness encroaches, sorrow holds calm
in each mother's heart, releases the promise
of no tomorrows. The women rest at the
base of the Virgin, weep for their
willful sons, the warmth of human
life against cold stone,
silent it ebbs away.

Gossip

Thunder rumbles all around the sea-side village. The lovers speed as swift as slugs compared to the spread of the news zig zagging like lightening across the full sky. Lips slaver and froth, mouths gnash, as wave after wave stirs the frenzied sea. The red dress flaps in all people's faces.

The blathering stops; takes a shower. A shovel bends over to pick up the sin. Trash cans clang; lids forced tight, and the village resumes its calm again

Swim Knitting

Cast on stiches, one by one
Swim the deep end
Purl and plain, back and forth
Breast stroke, butterfly, crawl.

Vest, sweater sleeve, scarf
What matters is the form
Click clack needles
Splish, splash, turn.

Inhale, exhale
Drop, add, loop
Ten laps to end the meet
Yarn unravels in a heap.

What if

Axle Alley

Yes, you can sing
huckleberry
the happy colour
life between lives

Channeled readings
wellspring visions
memory healings
soul repairs at axle alley

Screw Driver's Retreat

Spring ahead, spick and span
non-stick cook set
cool touch handles
indulge, share, repeat.

Cast-iron cookware
rustic charm meets
modern style
of disconnected life

Wireless heart rate
pressure cooker
weekend's warrior

Low and Slow
(Source: from the titles in *British Columbia's Knowledge Network Magazine* Nov/Dec 2017)

striking balance
hope for wildlife
joan of arc: god's warrior

planet oil
canada over the edge
the polar sea

the missing
heartbeat
silent witness

a park for all seasons
storyville – the
price of the American dream

death in paradise
blowdown
secrets from the sky

low and slow
monster moves
how many people can live on planet earth?

Pennies

He sat and smoked
on a stiff-backed chair
flung pennies
onto the floorboards
she picked them up
he licked his lips
flicked his butt

Crocheting Yoga

Ovum and sperm link and grow
Begins a chain with yarn and hook
Flow mountain into downward facing dog
Yarn over and draw through
Triangle, turn for warrior I and II

Alternate rows single and double
Hold, camel, lion, cobra
Circle, seed, shell, cluster
Balance, tree, crane, trunk of an elephant

Loop, drop, oops
Splayed legs collapse the head stand
Grannie square unravels – breathe –
Short distance between child's pose and corpse
Colonization and torment

Send Off

cranes clutter the skyline
she pulls on long white gloves

a gentle push on her back
like sex with the wind

Green Notebook

Flames flare from the stack
of the oil refinery, a shrine
without souvenirs.
Thoughts float loose
in his mind. "Life revolves
around money, power, and sex."
He takes a further
swig of beer, "Best be careful
what you write in that
green notebook of yours."

Risk

woodpeckers clatter
knock their brains
out for a grub

workers at week's end
risk all
in a poker game
the shallow pockets
of a pool table

milk and cream
sweet or sour

Fur Trimmed

For the want of a drink
a ride with celebrity
sucker for a pout.

He laughed,
want a ride girlie?

White figure skates
fur trimmed
rabbit down the well.

Capitalism

My knees tremble at the threat
of a consumer collapse.
I chuckle as politicians fiddle
while the planet burns.

I won't go easy.
I promise messy
when I fall.

Big Fat Purses

Sprawl poolside; raise glasses to starlight
Sup on succulent seafood delights

Landscapes boast of artificial petals
Free from patches of nettles

Trees cut down faster than they grow
Air pollutes; humans have no place to go

Drill and dig and frack; destroy the core
Abandon roots; close tight the ancient door

Hurry, hurry, get your share; feed your greed
Pay no heed to Mother Nature's need.

Dwindling

aromas of cinnamon and nutmeg
mixed with sour milk and mold
linger in mother earth's pantry
while bedroom life slows

she shuffles around on her axis
takes the last Kleenex, or perhaps
a Scotties, from the last tree
dabs at a tear near her dimple
high on her cheek

lowers onto a rotting wooden bench
and from a sliver of vision
watches the plastic tide roll in

What if

What if the farmer planted
rye instead of barley
drank whisky instead of beer
never traded his horses
for a John Deere
never smoked tailor-mades
instead of roll-your-owns

What if his wife served
frozen desserts
instead of hot biscuits

What if the food industry
produced food safe to eat

What if colonization
never occurred

Where Rests the Heart

Sugar and Lime
For Anthony

They sip Chablis in the glow of
candles. Eat prawns dipped in butter.
Spread a blanket with petals, and
feast on a fondue of delights. They

sleep, catching dreams from stars shining
through the window. Sip coffee in the
morning. But… the firewood is damp.
The stove goes out. The cat meows to be fed,

and a hornet buzzes between
the window and the screen. The telephone
rings and he… spills the sugar. She
brushes it away. He answers the phone

before stomping out. She sulks at
the sink. Later… they meet in the garden.
He winks and she smiles. They sprinkle
lime; an attempt to re-sweeten the soil.

Sofa in Spice

Seduce with rose,
heliotrope and cedar wood
use a radiant scent
of florals and warm vanilla
hints of lavender and musk
the sparkle of pear
peony and almond blossom
captivate senses with lemon,
cardamom, tonka bean,
a fiery blend of black coffee,
blood orange and ebony wood
bold shoulders and gum boots
on the sofa in spice.

Toothpaste

The Wednesday I woke up, and saw the glob
of toothpaste in the sink, and said how I
was fed up cleaning after someone
else, you huffed out the door.
My heart squeezed regret
with no chance to put
the toothpaste
back into
the tube
again.

Beach Slippers
For Richard

He once said with a grin on his face, "It's the shoes on our feet that carry us through."

And, I see him still, striding down the trail, with silly-city shoes on his feet. I sense his pause at my garden gate; his request for flowers for Kathleen.

A sea breeze beckons, and I walk towards his empty cabin; old running shoes on my feet. I place flowers, for Kathleen, under the Yew tree where two pairs of beach slippers sway.

Breakfast

With you…
Kelloggs bran flakes, sometimes
Quaker oatmeal, sprinkled with
psyllium husk and flax meal,
topped with blueberries and banana.

Table cleared for coffee,
cribbage, sometimes Skip-Bo.

Without you…
Quaker oatmeal, sometimes
Kelloggs bran flakes, sprinkled with
flax meal, topped with banana.

Table cluttered for ginger tea,
solitaire, cry to fill the empty.

Fly Swatter

A fly buzzes around me as I read in bed. It buzzes between my face and the page, around my head and against the wall. I reach for Mother's fly swatter with one hand. Hold my book with the other, wait, pretend to read, bored, I start to read. The fly buzzes on by – quick – it disappears before I can swat. I put the book down. Turn off the light. Silence, I turn the light back on. Buzzzzz, even before I pick the book up again. I leap out of bed, swatter in hand...no buzz, no fly... crawl back into bed.

That you Mother? Trying to tell me something?

But, my mother was never a fly. As a child, I saw her as a bee in the sweet-peas and sunshine. Busy, always, busy. She soothed us with honey whenever she could. By middle age, though, she was a grouse, tamed and submissive until the breakdown. She agreed to electric-shock treatment; but only once, perhaps twice, then hissed, "No more." Discharged herself. Crossed the bridge. Walked twenty-two blocks to get home again. Snarled and snapped until ninety-three; all along she was a wolverine.

One Breath

The road winds up the hill from St. Peter's College into Muenster village. It is snowing, it is windy, and slippery under foot. My backpack contains a scant change of clothing; pajamas and clean underwear, but still too heavy with the load of textbooks and my laptop. The 10:00 a.m. church bells interrupt the squeak and crunch under my snow boots. *These bells for me*, I mutter, *ringing in my 69th year*? Realty hits as I stumble and nearly fall crossing the cold steel of railway tracks.

Nothing is open in the village of Muenster on a Sunday morning. There is no warm shelter. I peer down highway number 5 towards Humboldt; no bus in sight. I turn my back to the wind, thinking I ought to take a closer look at Online Learning. My coat gets wet. A shiver runs up my spine.

Mother always told us never to get our clothes wet when outside in a Saskatchewan winter. *It is the worst thing that can happen*, she said, *you'll freeze to death and not even know it.*

My toes tingle; one side of my face feels numb. I stamp my feet; flap my arms. One breath – the measure between life and death – the arrival of European settlers.

Handkerchief

Made of cotton, I was white,
lightly starched, crocheted
lace around my edges.
Ironed, and folded
into a triangle to represent
the three persons in one God.

She placed me on top
of her little white prayer book,
and clasped us in her hands.

I felt a tremble when she
opened her mouth, stuck out
her tongue, and received
Holy Communion for the first time.

Communion faltered during the time
she was a teenager, and I found
myself stuffed into the back
of a dresser drawer, crumpled
and stained with lipstick, chocolate
ice cream, orange crush, dried
snot, and tears.

Now I rest on the corner of her
night table in the nursing home.
My crocheted lace frayed. I am grey.
The stains faded, I'm unstarched,
unironed, folded into a rectangle,
the shape of a grave.

Night Waters

Off-the-grid we had an outhouse
At night we used a bucket.

Diluted our night waters
for watering –
    bamboo
      clematis
        wisteria

Never used it on edibles
except for rhubarb
which we mostly never ate.

In-the-city our hearts filled
with homesick –
    flush
      flush
        flush

Where Rests the Heart

From the hand-crafted house, at the edge of the forest
by the side of the Salish Sea,
I gaze upon the sparkling waters, and
snow crowned Beaufort Mountains.
I stand still, to hear the tidal change, the bark of seals,
the wind as it whispers through Douglas fir.

But come springtime, I'm eager to hit the road,
to get to the other side of Hope.
and return to Saskatchewan,
the *Land of the Living Skies*
hear the Meadowlark's song,
stare into the inky-blue sloughs,
see new crops in the fields, admire again,
the caragana hedge; the Russian thistle.

I tell him winter on the Prairies is a serious
matter – snow tires, block heaters, ice scrapers,
shovels, snow blowers, and even roof-rakes
to remove snow off the roofs of houses.

I tell him it's a place where you can freeze to death
if your car leaves the road, and no one notices
that you're stuck in a ditch.

And yes, winter is a serious matter
when we move back. For all of his bravado,
I shovel most of the snow the first winter.
I don't really mind the snow and the cold
but I mind that it lasts for so long.

I mind that the lakes and rivers freeze.
I miss the open water.
I long for the sight of the sea,
the tide going in and out,
the smell of the salt,
a cloud at rest on a mountain.

Acknowledgements

My thanks to the editors of the following magazines, who first published some of these poems, sometimes in earlier versions.

Blue Cubicle Press: "A Higher Social Level" 2020
Spring: "Coyotes" 2015
The Society: "Toothpaste" 2013; "Breakfast" 2016
Portal: "Shucking" 2015
Transition: "Battleford" 2015
Ascent Aspirations Magazine: "Cultivated Time" May 2018
Soft Cartel: "Contrition," "At the Convent of St. Katherina," "Night Waters" June 2018
Eskimo Pie Magazine: "Winter," "Dying Blue," "Crocheting Yoga," "Swim Knitting," "Sofa in Spice" Nov. 2018
Indolent Arts: "Capitalism" 2018; "Dwindling" April 2020
Tisdale Writers Group Inc.: "Hands of a Working Man" 2013; "Another Cigarette" 2014

Versions of some poems have appeared in *Celebrating Our Writers; Lasqueti Arts Festival Anthologies*: 2002, 2003, 2004.

I would like to thank Robert Hilles, poet and professor at Vancouver Island University for his unending patience, support, and encouragement to complete this poetry collection. My heartfelt appreciation goes to Barbara Langhorst, Candice Savage, and St. Peter's College in Muenster, Saskatchewan, for whetting my appetite for university courses in creative writing. I am grateful to Sue Wheeler and the Lasqueti Writers' Group who got me into writing poetry whether I wanted to or not. Thanks to Anthony Hutchins for reading my many poetry drafts and always being there for me. Thanks, as well, to family, friends, and the different communities I have lived in for providing an abundant supply of inspirational material for me to work from.

About the Author

Photo courtesy of Anthony Hutchins

Rose Willow is the author of three poetry chapbooks: *Shucking, Relief Train,* and *Anguish*. She has written articles for *Horticulture Magazine, Saskatchewan History Magazine,* and *Incline*.

She grew up in Saskatchewan, moved west as a young adult, and met the love of her life. Together they embraced an off-the-grid lifestyle on Lasqueti Island where they built a small house at the edge of the forest by the side of the sea. While there, Rose completed a History degree through the University of Waterloo distance education program.

She now lives in Parksville, BC, and recently completed a Bachelor of Arts degree in Creative Writing "with Distinction" at Vancouver Island University.

www.ingramcontent.com/pod-product-compliance
Lightning Source LLC
Chambersburg PA
CBHW050445010526
44118CB00013B/1683